The Truth (and Myths) About the Presidents

by L. A. Peacock
Illustrated by Nick Wigsby

Scholastic Inc.

To Steven, Rob, and Dudley—with love—L.A.F.

Thank you to the following for their kind permission to use their photographs in this book:

9 middle: Wikipedia; 10 top: Library of Congress/neg.#DIG-pga-01368; 11 middle: © North Wind/North Wind Picture Archives; 14 top: Library of Congress/neg.#LC-USZC4-7933; 15 top: Library of Congress/neg.#LC-H8- C01-104-A; 16 bottom: The Granger Collection, NYC; 18 top: Library of Congress/neg.#DIG-ppmsca-30581; 19 top: Library of Congress/neg.#LC-DIG-ppmsca-30581; 20 top: Library of Congress/neg.# 3g05801u; 21 top: Library of Congress/neg.#LC-USZC4-2109; 23 top: Library of Congress/neg.#LC-USZ62-95455; 24 top: Library of Congress/neg.#LC-USZ62-95455; 25 top: Library of Congress/neg.#LC-USZC2-2715; 26 top: Library of Congress/neg.# LC-USZ62-1491; 27 top: Library of Congress/neg.#LC-USZ62-1301; 28 top: Library of Congress/neg.#LC-DIG-cwpbh-0069; 29 top: Library of Congress/neg.# LC-USZC2-2424; 30 top: Library of Congress/neg.#LC-USZC4-10080; 30 bottom: AP Images; 31 top: Library of Congress/neg.# LC-DIG-ppmsca-19241; 32 bottom: National Portrait Gallery, Smithsonian Institution, Washington, DC; 35 top: Library of Congress/neg.#LC-DIG-ppmsca-05704; 36 top: Library of Congress/neg.# LC-USZC4-678; 37 top: Library of Congress/neg.#LC-DIG-pga-01375; 38 top: Library of Congress/neg.# LC-DIG-pga-01369; 39 top: Library of Congress/neg.#LC-USZ62-13021; 40 top: Library of Congress/neg.# LC-USZ62-48559; 42 top: Library of Congress/neg.#LC-USZ62-134885; 43 top: Library of Congress/neg.#LC-USZ62-117982; 44 top: Library of Congress/neg.#LC-USZC4-11548; 44 bottom: Library of Congress/neg.#LC-DIG-stereo-1s02115; 48 top: Library of Congress/neg.#LC-USZC2-6278; 49 center: AP Images; 50 top: Library of Congress/neg.# LC-USZC2-6247; 52 top: Library of Congress/neg.#LC-DIG-hec-18303; 53 top: Library of Congress/neg.# LC-DIG-ppmsc-03670; 54 top: Library of Congress/neg.#LC-DIG-hec-18540; 54 bottom left: Corbis; 54 bottom right: The Granger Collection, NYC; 55 top: Library of Congress/neg.#LC-USZ62-117121; 56 center: AP Images; 57 bottom left: Corbis; 57 bottom right: Corbis; 59 top: Library of Congress/neg.#LC-USZ62-117122; 60 center: Rue des Archives/ The Granger Collection, NYC; 61 top: Library of Congress/neg.#LC-USZ62-117124; 61 center: AP Photo; 63 top: Library of Congress/neg.# LOC_LC-USZ62-117124; 64 bottom: Cecil Staughton/Newscom; 65: AP Photo; 66 top: Lyndon Baines Johnson Presidential Library; 66 center: John F. Kennedy Presidential Library, Boston; 68 top: Library of Congress/neg.#LC-USZ62-13037; 70 top: Gerald R. Ford Presidential Library; 71 top: Jimmy Carter Library and Museum; 72 top: Ronald Reagan Presidential Library; 72 center: David Levenson/Hulton Archives/Getty Images; 73 bottom: AP Images; 74 top: George Bush Presidential Library; 76 top: William J. Clinton Presidential Library; 77 bottom: Bryan Snyder/Reuters; 78 bottom: Reuters; 79 top: George W. Bush Presidential Library; 80 bottom: Stephen Jaffe/AFP/Getty Images/Newscom; 82 top: Library of Congress/neg.#LC-DIG-ppbd-00358; 82 bottom: Chris Keane/Reuters.

ISBN 978-0-545-56848-7

Text copyright © 2014 by L. A. Peacock
Illustrations copyright © 2014 by Scholastic Inc.

12 11 10 9 8 7 6 5 4 3 2   14 15 16 17 18 19/0

Printed in the U. S. A.   40

First edition, January 2014

 Contents

☆ ☆ ☆ ☆ ☆ ☆ ☆ ☆ ☆ ☆ ☆

About the President

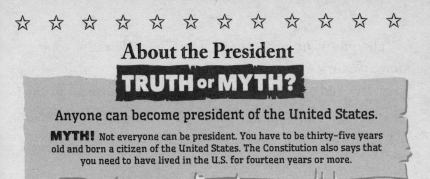

TRUTH or MYTH?

Anyone can become president of the United States.

MYTH! Not everyone can be president. You have to be thirty-five years old and born a citizen of the United States. The Constitution also says that you need to have lived in the U.S. for fourteen years or more.

What's the president's job?

ELECT ME

The president is the chief executive of the United States. It's a big job, maybe the toughest in the world. The president is a powerful leader, because the U.S. has the world's largest economy.

At the beginning of each year, the president gives his or her plan for the coming year in the State of the Union speech. Congress votes on bills, or new laws, that the president proposes. Congress can also pass its own laws. The president has **veto** power to stop Congress from acting.

THE *AYES* HAVE IT! THE BILL IS PASSED.

The president is in charge of foreign policy and appoints **ambassadors** to other countries. Treaties are signed by the president and approved by the Senate. As commander in chief of the armed forces, the president is head of all branches of the military.

Supreme Court justices and other high court judges are appointed by the president. Cabinet members are also chosen by the president. These officials must be approved by the Senate. Other important positions that are required to run the government can be filled under the president's power alone.

How often is there a presidential election?

Every four years. Political parties nominate candidates for president. There is a long campaign so voters can get to know the candidates before making a decision. Some states have **primary elections** before the national election in November. The president is elected to a four-year term. No president is allowed to serve more than two terms.

How is the president elected?

Not directly by the people. When voting for a candidate for president, the voters in each state choose an **elector**, who promises to vote for their candidate. (The number of electors in each state is equal to the number of senators and representatives that state has in Congress.) All electors together make up the Electoral College.

In most states, the candidate who gets the most votes wins the state's electoral vote. After the election, the Electoral College meets. The electors choose the president by majority vote.

Could *you* vote for president?

Only if you are a U.S. citizen and at least eighteen years old. But first, you have to register to vote, usually at the city or town hall where you live.

When does the president take the oath of office?

At noon on January 20 following the election. The **inauguration** ceremony takes place on the steps of the U.S. Capitol. The president-elect puts one hand on a Bible and raises the other hand and makes a promise to the nation.

The Chief Justice of the Supreme Court administers this **oath** of office:

"I do solemnly swear that I will faithfully execute the office of President of the United States, and will, to the best of my ability, preserve, protect, and defend the Constitution of the United States."

☆ ☆ ☆ ☆ ☆ ☆ ☆ ☆ ☆ ☆ ☆ ☆

Meet the Presidents

George Washington
1789–1797

Who was America's first president?

George Washington. He was a famous general and Revolutionary War hero. As Commander of the Continental Army, Washington led the fight to win America's **independence** from England. After the war, he was everyone's choice to head the new republic.

How did Washington learn to be a soldier?

At twenty-one, Washington joined the military. The American colonies belonged to England at the time. Washington helped the British win the French and Indian War. He knew how to fight in the wilderness, and led surprise attacks against the French army. Later, soldiers during the American Revolution used this strategy to defeat the British.

Was George Washington a great general?

Yes, but not because of his success in battle. In fact, his army lost more battles than it won! Washington's greatness was his ability to inspire and lead his men.

How did Washington celebrate Christmas in 1776?

By crossing the Delaware River in secret. It was the middle of the Revolutionary War. General Washington led his 2,400-man army across the icy river on the dark night of December 25. The British were defeated in the surprise attack on Trenton, New Jersey. The battle turned the tide of the war for the American patriots.

Why didn't George Washington smile a lot?

He wore false teeth, which hurt. Washington had lost most of his own teeth from gum disease before he was thirty. His false teeth were made from elephant and walrus tusks and held together by steel springs and wires. Washington had to press down hard to keep his mouth closed!

TRUTH or MYTH?

George Washington chopped down a cherry tree when he was six.

MYTH! This story was made up as a lesson for children, to show how honest he was. "I cannot tell a lie. I did it with my hatchet," said young George to his father in the tale.

OOPS!

TRUTH or MYTH?

Washington was the only president to have a state named after him.

TRUTH! As the first president, Washington has his name and image on everything from the dollar bill to postage stamps.

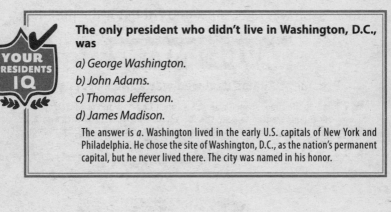

YOUR PRESIDENTS IQ

The only president who didn't live in Washington, D.C., was

a) George Washington.

b) John Adams.

c) Thomas Jefferson.

d) James Madison.

The answer is *a*. Washington lived in the early U.S. capitals of New York and Philadelphia. He chose the site of Washington, D.C., as the nation's permanent capital, but he never lived there. The city was named in his honor.

THEY STARTED BUILDING THE WHITE HOUSE IN 1792.

JOHN ADAMS WAS THE FIRST PRESIDENT TO LIVE THERE.

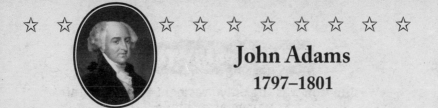

John Adams
1797–1801

Did John Adams want to run for president?

Yes. Adams had served as Washington's vice president, but he wasn't happy in that job. Adams was a talker, and the vice president's job was to be quiet and fill in for the president.

TRUTH or MYTH?

President Adams declared war against France.

MYTH! At the time, France was at war with England and other European nations. But Adams wanted to keep the U.S. out of war. To keep America safe, he ordered warships to be built. The first great battleship, the USS *Constitution*, was launched in 1797.

ADAMS WAS CALLED "THE FATHER OF THE U.S. NAVY."

Where did First Lady Abigail Adams hang her laundry?

In the East Room of the White House. The Adams family was the first to live in the "President's House." The walls were still wet with paint when they called it home in 1800.

Thomas Jefferson
1801–1809

What did Jefferson send George III, the British king, in 1776?

The Declaration of Independence. Jefferson was the main author of this historic **document**. He wrote that the American colonists were free of British rule and had the rights to life, liberty, and the pursuit of happiness: "We hold these truths to be self-evident, that all men are created equal."

How did Jefferson show he was "a man of the people"?

He dressed and acted like everyone else. He stopped putting powder in his hair, like rich people did. Jefferson wore plain clothes and walked to work from his home to the Capitol building. On New Year's Day, he invited ordinary citizens to visit the White House.

Jefferson had many talents:

- He knew six languages.
- He founded the University of Virginia.
- He designed Monticello, his home in Charlottesville, Virginia.
- He was a scientist, **naturalist**, and brilliant writer.
- He danced, sang, and played the violin.

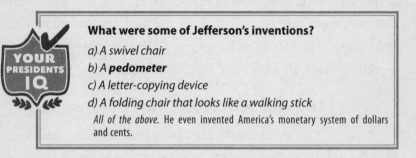

What were some of Jefferson's inventions?

a) A swivel chair
*b) A **pedometer***
c) A letter-copying device
d) A folding chair that looks like a walking stick

All of the above. He even invented America's monetary system of dollars and cents.

Jefferson's Polygraph: This device copies a letter as it is written.

How did Jefferson double the size of the United States?

By buying a big chunk of land from France for $15 million. This deal was called the "Louisiana Purchase." Jefferson asked Meriwether Lewis and William Clark to explore the new territory west of the Mississippi River. Lewis and Clark sent the president new animals they discovered, including prairie dogs and two grizzly bears.

What happened on July 4, fifty years after the Declaration of Independence was signed?

Both Thomas Jefferson and John Adams, two of America's Founding Fathers, died hours apart on the same historic date in 1826.

James Madison
1808–1817

How did Madison earn the nickname "Father of the Constitution"?

He authored the Bill of Rights, guaranteeing all Americans freedoms of speech, religion, **assembly**, and the right to trial by jury.

What was "Mr. Madison's War"?

The U.S. fought the War of 1812 against the British over the kidnapping of American sailors. The war ended with the American victory in the Battle of New Orleans. A peace treaty was signed in 1815.

TRUTH or MYTH?

Washington, D.C., was badly burned in 1814.

TRUTH! British troops set the capital city on fire. First Lady Dolley Madison saved important papers and a famous painting of George Washington from the burning White House.

James Monro

1817–1825

TRUTH or MYTH?

President Monroe was a school "dropout."

TRUTH! He left college to fight in the Revolutionary War. Monroe crossed the Delaware with General Washington's army on Christmas night, 1776, and was wounded.

THE U.S. GOT A LOT BIGGER UNDER MONROE.

FIVE NEW STATES, AND HE BOUGHT FLORIDA FROM SPAIN.

MAP

Was Monroe a popular president?

Yes. He served two terms. Only Washington previously had received more electoral votes. Monroe was cheered everywhere he went. It was an "era of good feeling."

What warning did Monroe send to European countries?

The Monroe Doctrine. The president told European leaders that no new colonies could be started in the Americas.

19

John Quincy Adams
1825–1829

Was the sixth president related to the second?

Yes, they were father and son. Young John Quincy traveled with his father, John Adams, to France during the Revolutionary War. Years later, John Quincy was sent by President Washington to represent the new nation as ambassador to several European countries.

TRUTH or MYTH?

John Quincy Adams liked to exercise every day.

TRUTH! He often left the White House and took long walks alone. In the early morning, he swam in the Potomac River, usually naked. One time, someone stole his clothes!

Was he a successful president?

Not really. Many people didn't like John Quincy Adams or his ideas for spending tax dollars to build roads and canals. He was not reelected for a second term.

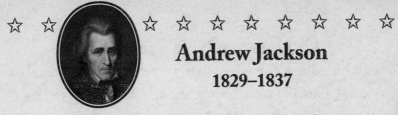

Andrew Jackson
1829–1837

Who was the first president born in a log cabin?

Andrew Jackson. As a "man of the people" and hero of the War of 1812, he was different from past presidents. Jackson was less educated, and his parents were poor and moved around a lot. He was born somewhere in the Carolinas, but we're not sure exactly where.

How did Jackson bring "frontier spirit" to the White House?

It started with his inauguration party. More than twenty thousand supporters crashed through the White House doors in wild celebration. The new president escaped from the crowd. He ended up spending the night in a hotel.

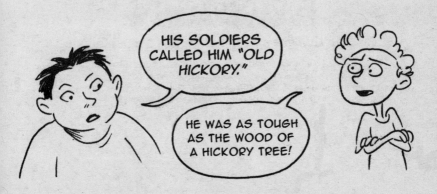

Did Jackson have a temper?

Yes, and he didn't turn the other cheek! Once, Jackson shot and killed a man in a duel when the man insulted his wife.

What was meant by "Jacksonian Democracy"?

Jackson promised to represent ordinary people. He used his power to veto, or reject, any laws from Congress that helped rich Americans. The people loved Jackson, and he was easily elected to a second term.

Why was Jackson called "King Andrew" by his critics?

They thought he had too much power. Jackson fired cabinet members who didn't follow his orders. He defied the Supreme Court and gave jobs to political supporters. He sometimes acted more like a king than an elected president.

TRUTH or MYTH?

Jackson thought a good Indian was a dead Indian.

TRUTH! He fought many battles against Native Americans when he was a soldier. The Creek Indians called him "Sharp Knife." As president, Jackson signed the Indian Removal Act of 1830. This law forced Native Americans to move from their homes to lands west of the Mississippi.

Martin Van Buren
1837–1841

Why was Van Buren known as the "O.K." candidate?

His birthplace was Kinderhook, New York. The O.K. Club was formed there after "Old Kinderhook," a Van Buren nickname. Later, "O.K." came to mean "all right."

TRUTH or MYTH?

Van Buren improved Andrew Jackson's Indian policies.

MYTH! No, he made it worse for more Native Americans. From 1838 to 1839, more than fifteen thousand Cherokee Indians were forced to march from their Georgia home to reservations in faraway Oklahoma. Many died along the way on this "Trail of Tears."

Was the "Little Magician" a popular president?

Van Buren, nicknamed by some the "Little Magician," was clever, like a fox. But he had little magic to figure out how to get the country out of economic trouble. Thousands lost their jobs when banks failed and businesses closed in the **Panic** of 1837. Voters blamed Van Buren. He wasn't reelected.

William Henry Harrison
1841

How many jobs did Harrison have before becoming president?

A lot. He studied to be a doctor, but he quit school to join the army. Harrison became an Indian fighter on the frontier. He led a thousand soldiers against Chief Tecumseh of the Shawnee Indians at the Tippecanoe River in 1811. Later, Harrison became a farmer and congressman. He ran for president as a war hero with the nickname "Old Tippecanoe."

How long was Harrison's presidency?

Only one month. Harrison had the shortest term in office of any president. But he gave the longest Inaugural Address at one hour and forty minutes! It was a cold day, and Harrison wasn't wearing a hat or a coat. He caught a bad cold. A few weeks later, the new president got pneumonia and died.

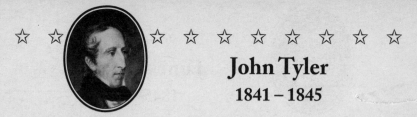

John Tyler
1841–1845

Why was Tyler called "His Accidency"?

When Harrison died, John Tyler became the first vice president to take over when a president died. Right away, he acted like a true president, showing he was no "accident." Tyler quickly took the oath of office, moved into the White House, and gave an Inaugural Address. He set an example for future vice presidents on how to take power.

Did Tyler like children?

Yes, because he had fifteen children of his own by two wives!

How did Tyler lose his job?

He didn't believe in his party's policies of high taxes and big government, so party bosses threw him out. Without a **political party**, Tyler didn't try to get reelected.

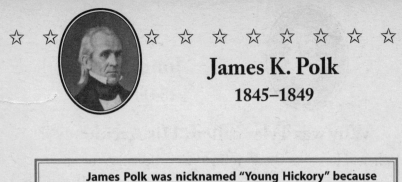

James K. Polk
1845–1849

What happened when Polk arrived at his Inaugural Ball?

The dancing ended. Polk's wife, Sarah, was very religious. She didn't believe in dancing, drinking, or card playing.

How did the U.S. grow under Polk?

Polk extended the U.S. boundaries to the Pacific Coast. He added the new states of Washington and Oregon by settling the border with Canada. He bought land from Mexico to create California, New Mexico, Arizona, Utah, Nevada, and parts of Colorado and Wyoming. In all, Polk added 1.2 million square miles of land to expand U.S. borders from "coast to coast."

Zachary Taylor
1849–1850

Why was Zachary Taylor nicknamed "Old Rough and Ready"?

Taylor was a soldier for forty years. His troops gave him that nickname. Taylor was a popular hero of the Mexican War. In one battle, he defeated an army four times bigger than his own!

Taylor often wore a straw hat and dirty clothes. He looked more like a farmer than a president. Visitors could see his horse Whitey grazing on the White House lawn.

TRUTH or MYTH?

The presidency was the first election Zachary Taylor ever won.

TRUTH! The election of 1848 was his first. In fact, he had never even voted before!

How prepared was Taylor to be president?

Taylor was a soldier, not a politician. The country was divided. The new territories in the West wanted to become states. Congress disagreed on whether to allow slavery in these new states. Politicians from the South began to talk about leaving the Union. Taylor wanted to keep the peace. Congress worked out a **compromise** on the slavery question.

Millard Fillmore
1850–1853

Did President Fillmore go to college?

No. He was born in a log cabin and didn't go to school. He taught himself to be a lawyer.

How did trade with Japan begin?

Fillmore sent Commodore Matthew Perry to Japan in 1853. After two hundred years of **isolation**, the Japanese emperor agreed to open trade links with other countries.

What did Fillmore do that pushed the U.S. toward civil war?

He signed the Fugitive Slave Act. This law required runaway slaves to be returned to their owners. Harriet Beecher Stowe, an **abolitionist**, was so angry that she wrote *Uncle Tom's Cabin*. This book showed the evils of slavery. It sold millions of copies and ignited antislavery feelings that swept the North.

Franklin Pierce
1853–1857

What tragedy happened to the Pierce family just before the president took office?

The president's eleven-year-old son, Benjamin, was killed in a train crash.

Did Pierce get more land for the U.S.?

Yes, he bought a piece of land from Mexico. Today this territory forms parts of New Mexico and Arizona.

How did Pierce move the country closer to civil war?

Pierce supported a law that let the people decide whether to allow slavery in their state. The result was "Bleeding Kansas." People fought over whether Kansas should become a "free state" or a "slave state."

☆ ☆  ☆ ☆ ☆ ☆ ☆ ☆ ☆ ☆

James Buchanan
1857–1861

Why did Buchanan support the Dred Scott decision?

The Supreme Court said that a slave, Dred Scott, was not a free man just because his owner moved him from a slave state to a free state.

The Supreme Court said slaves were property, not free citizens. Slave owners were pleased, but the North was furious. John Brown, a **radical** abolitionist, raided Harpers Ferry, Virginia. Brown wanted to attack slave owners in the South, but he was captured and hanged.

What did Buchanan do after the raid on Harpers Ferry?

He sent federal troops to arrest Frederick Douglass, a former slave and abolitionist leader. Abolitionists in the North were angry. Events were getting out of control. One after another, seven Southern states left the Union.

30

Abraham Lincoln
1861–1865

What did Lincoln carry with him when he ran for president?

A wooden ax. It reminded voters of Lincoln's early job as a rail splitter. Lincoln was born in a log cabin on the frontier. His family was poor, so he went to school for only one year. Lincoln taught himself to be a lawyer. He borrowed books and read all the time, even when on horseback.

YOUR PRESIDENTS IQ

Lincoln held many jobs, including:

a) ferryboat captain.

b) surveyor.

c) store clerk.

d) postmaster.

e) lawyer.

All of the above. He was also elected to the U.S. House of Representatives before running for president in 1860.

What did Lincoln look like?

He was tall, thin, and awkward looking. His clothes did not fit well. At six feet four inches, Lincoln was our tallest president. His voice was high-pitched. Lincoln had a gift for storytelling. People liked him, and he could make them laugh.

What sad events happened to Lincoln's family?

The president and Mrs. Lincoln had four sons. The oldest, Robert, was away at school. The second oldest, Edward, died in 1850 at the age of three. Lincoln often wrestled with his two youngest sons, Willie and Tad, on the White House floor.

But tragedy struck in 1862 when young Willie died from typhoid fever. He was the only child to die in the White House. Tad died a few years later.

What did Lincoln promise to do
at his first inauguration?

He took the oath to "preserve, protect, and defend the Union."
But eleven Southern states had broken away and formed the
Confederate States of America. They wanted to keep slavery
and their way of life. Soon after, the Civil War began.

Which side was winning the war
in the early fighting?

At first, the South had more victories. But the North turned
the tide by winning the Battle of Gettysburg in 1863. At
Gettysburg, more than fifty-one
thousand soldiers were killed,
wounded, or missing. Lincoln
gave his famous speech at the
dedication of a cemetery on
that battlefield. By the end of
the Civil War in 1865, six
hundred thousand men had
been killed.

How was Lincoln able to free the slaves?

He declared the end of slavery in the Confederate states when he issued the **Emancipation Proclamation** in 1863. The Thirteenth **Amendment** to the Constitution, passed after the Civil War ended, freed the slaves as the official law of the land.

Did Lincoln live to see the end of the Civil War?

Yes, but just barely. Five days after the war ended, Lincoln was shot by John Wilkes Booth while watching a play at Ford's Theatre in Washington, D.C. Lincoln was the first president to be **assassinated**, or killed, in office. The nation mourned the loss of this great leader.

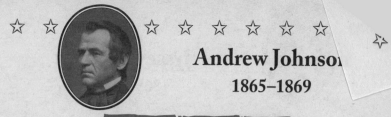

Andrew Johnson
1865–1869

Why was Johnson put on trial?

Many in Congress disagreed with Johnson's political views and tried to remove him from office. They voted to **impeach** him and put him on trial. They thought he was "too easy" on the South. But Congress failed to convict Johnson by one vote, so he stayed in office and completed his term.

Who taught the president how to read?

His wife, Eliza, taught him how to read and write. Johnson never went to school. But he could sew. He became a tailor.

JOHNSON WAS THE ONLY EX-PRESIDENT ELECTED TO THE SENATE.

Ulysses S. Grant
1869–1877

How good a horseman was Grant?

A good one. Grant loved horses since he was a kid. At the age of five, he could ride standing up in the saddle.

Did Grant get into trouble with the law?

The president was stopped for speeding in his horse-drawn carriage. The police officer took his vehicle, so Grant had to walk back to the White House.

Rutherford B. Hayes
1877–1881

Why did Congress, not the voters, decide the presidential election of 1876?

The election was too close to call. There was fraud in counting the votes, so Congress had to decide the results. In the end, Hayes won by one electoral vote.

Lucy Hayes became famous as First Lady because she:

a) was the first First Lady to cancel the inaugural ball.

b) served soft drinks, not alcohol, at the White House.

c) held Easter Egg Rolls on the White House lawn.

d) invited Thomas Edison to play his new phonograph for the president.

The answers are *b*, *c*, and *d*. She was known as "Lemonade Lucy." The First Lady was a supporter of the **temperance** movement that wanted to ban all alcoholic drinks.

Whose phone number was "1"?

The president's. Hayes was the first president to use a phone in the White House. Inventor Alexander Graham Bell personally installed the phone.

RIIIIIING!!!

NUMBER 1 IS NOT HERE RIGHT NOW. LEAVE YOUR MESSAGE AT THE BEEP.

James A. Garfield
1881

How long did Garfield serve as president?

Only four months. He was shot on July 2, 1881, at a Washington, D.C., train station. The assassin was angry because he could not get a government job. Ten weeks later, Garfield died of the gunshot wound. He was the fourth president to die in office.

Garfield was a teacher. Why did he choose this career?

He actually wanted to be a sailor, but he fell off a boat and nearly drowned. Later, he became a teacher, professor, and college president.

HAVE YOU SEEN JAMES?

How did Garfield sign his name?

With both hands. He was ambidextrous, or able to write with either hand.

Chester A. Arthur
1881–1885

Why was Chester Arthur known as "Elegant Arthur"?

He was a fancy dresser. Arthur changed his clothes several times a day for different White House events. He was the first president to hire a valet to take care of his clothes and to help him dress.

ARTHUR OWNED EIGHTY PAIRS OF PANTS!

How did Arthur anger his supporters?

People now had to earn their government jobs. Arthur established the **Civil Service** Commission. The president refused to give old friends government jobs until they passed an exam to show they were qualified. Once in the job, a person couldn't be fired when another president took office.

What sport did the president excel in?

Fishing. He once caught an eighty-pound bass off the Rhode Island coast.

Grover Cleveland
1885–1889, 1893–1897

TRUTH or MYTH?

Cleveland served three terms as president.

MYTH! He served two terms, but they weren't two terms in a row. Cleveland was kicked out of office in 1889, but returned as president four years later. He was the only president to serve two terms that did not follow each other.

WE'LL BE BACK!

What government job *didn't* Cleveland have?

a) County sheriff

b) Mayor

c) Governor

d) Vice president

The answer is *d*. It took only eleven years for Cleveland to go from local sheriff to president of the United States.

YOUR PRESIDENTS IQ

CLEVELAND WEIGHED 250 POUNDS.

HE WAS NICKNAMED "UNCLE JUMBO"!

What big White House event marked Cleveland's first term?

A wedding—*his*! Cleveland married Frances Folsom. At twenty-one, she was the youngest first lady ever. Their second child, Esther, was the first child of a president to be born in the White House. Their first child, nicknamed "Baby Ruth," had a candy bar named after her.

Where did the president disappear to during a vacation in 1893?

He sneaked aboard a private yacht and had mouth surgery. The doctors removed a tumor and part of his jaw. They put in a piece of rubber for the missing bone. There were no scars. It took twenty-four years before anyone found out about the operation.

Benjamin Harrison
1889–1893

Who was Benjamin Harrison's famous relative?

His grandfather William Henry Harrison was the ninth president. "Little Ben" grew up on the family's farm in Ohio. "Grandfather's hat fits!" declared the five-foot-six-inch Harrison, as he campaigned for president in 1888.

Did Harrison have a "warm and fuzzy" personality?

No, just the opposite. People found Harrison cold and unfriendly, earning him the nickname the "Human Iceberg."

How did President Harrison welcome new immigrants to the U.S.?

He opened New York's Ellis Island in 1892. Millions of new citizens from Europe were processed there when they arrived in the U.S. **Immigrants** often took low-paying jobs and worked long hours in American factories. They blamed the president for their hard lives and voted him out of office.

William McKinley
1897–1901

TRUTH or MYTH?

President McKinley didn't like to shave.

MYTH! He was clean-shaven. In fact, he was the first president since Andrew Johnson not to have a beard or mustache.

Why was McKinley the first "high-tech" president?

He brought the presidency into the modern age. McKinley used the telephone and telegraph regularly. The White House could communicate easily with government departments.

How did McKinley expand U.S. influence around the world?

He fought a four-month war with Spain in 1898 that put Cuba, Puerto Rico, Guam, and the Philippines under U.S. control. The president took over the Hawaiian Islands and on July 7, 1898, Hawaii became an official territory. Under McKinley, the U.S. became a **global** power.

Did McKinley complete his second term?

No. On September 6, 1901, he was shot by an assassin as he reached out to shake hands in a crowd.

Theodore Roosevelt
1901–1909

How old was Theodore Roosevelt when he became president?

He was forty-two, the youngest president ever. He took over when McKinley was assassinated in 1901.

Was the president an active child?

Young Teddy had asthma and was sickly. But he exercised a lot. In college, Roosevelt was a champion boxer. After his mother and wife died hours apart on the same day in 1884, Roosevelt bought a ranch out west and he worked as a cowboy.

When did Roosevelt become a "Rough Rider"?

He organized a group of horsemen during the Spanish-American War. He led them on a dangerous charge to take Cuba's San Juan Hill.

How did Roosevelt work to protect the working poor from big business?

He wanted a "Square Deal" for everyone. He passed laws to break up the power of **monopolies**, or companies that were so big that they unfairly controlled the prices of their products

Roosevelt knew workers and small businesses needed protection. He supported laws to increase safe ways to prepare medicine, meats, and other food products.

Why did cartoons show Roosevelt carrying a "big stick"?

The big stick was a symbol of his foreign policy. The U.S. acted as police officer around the globe under Roosevelt. The president won the **Nobel Prize** for Peace in 1905 when he negotiated the end of the war between Russia and Japan.

Who "took over" the White House when Roosevelt was president?

His six kids. Called the "White House Gang" by reporters, Roosevelt's wild sons were always causing trouble. They chased pets and slid down staircases on dinner trays. They took their ponies up and down the White House elevators and roller-skated in the hallways. The president's popular daughter Alice had a pet snake and even smoked in public!

Did President Roosevelt invent the Teddy Bear?

No. A toy maker did! A man heard that the president had saved the life of a bear on a hunting trip. He named his stuffed bear after "Teddy's bear."

TEDDY BEAR ON SALE HERE

Roosevelt was a conservationist and protector of the environment.

TRUTH! The president set aside millions of acres of the country's natural forest for resource development and established five national parks. After he retired, Roosevelt went on safari in Africa and collected hundreds of animals for the Smithsonian museums.

What famous man did Roosevelt invite to dinner at the White House?

Booker T. Washington. He was the first African-American to receive an invitation to dine with a president.

YOUR PRESIDENTS IQ

Roosevelt was the first president in office to ride by:

a) car.

b) train.

c) submarine.

d) plane.

The answers are *a* and *c*. After he left office, Roosevelt became the first president to ride in an airplane.

William Howard Taft
1909–1913

Was he really the heaviest president ever?

Yes. At 332 pounds, William Howard Taft holds the record. He even had a special oversize bathtub built at the White House after he got stuck in a regular-sized one!

TRUTH or MYTH?

Taft took frequent rests from his presidential duties.

TRUTH! He was so relaxed that he even fell asleep at official events. Once, he slept through a parade in his honor through the streets of New York City.

TAFT KEPT COWS ON THE WHITE HOUSE LAWN!

Why should Americans think of Taft every April?

He was responsible for the Sixteenth Amendment requiring all U.S. citizens to pay income taxes.

What was Taft's favorite sport?

Baseball. He was a pretty good hitter. Taft started the presidential tradition of throwing out the first ball on opening day of the baseball season.

How did Taft end his political career?

As Chief Justice of the Supreme Court. Taft was appointed to the Court after serving as president. He wrote 253 court opinions and served for nine years on the bench.

Where was Taft laid to rest after his death?

Taft was the first president to be buried in Arlington National Cemetery. His wife, Helen, was buried with him thirteen years later. John F. Kennedy and his wife, Jackie, are the only other presidential couple buried at Arlington.

Woodrow Wilson
1913–1921

What did President Wilson work hard to prevent?

He tried to keep the U.S. out of World War I, which began in Europe in 1914. But in 1917, when German submarines sank U.S. ships, Wilson entered the U.S. into the war. The "Great War" ended eighteen months later.

Wilson went to Paris to negotiate the peace and to start the League of Nations. But Congress stopped the U.S. from joining the League. Wilson earned the Nobel Peace Prize for his efforts. Twenty-five years later, the United Nations took the place of the League as a place for settling disagreements among nations.

YOUR PRESIDENTS IQ

American citizens helped win the war with a country-wide *rationing* program, including

a) not eating meat on Mondays.

b) going without gas for their cars on Sundays.

c) brushing their teeth once a day.

d) drinking tea instead of coffee.

The answers are *a* and *b*. The Wilsons tried to save gas by using sheep, instead of machines, to "mow" the White House lawn!

Did Wilson like to read?

Yes, but he had a hard time decoding letters on the page. Wilson struggled with dyslexia, a learning disability. It took him longer to learn to read and write, but Wilson went on to graduate from college. He became a professor and college president.

Why did women like Wilson?

He supported many of their causes. Wilson passed laws against child labor and called for an eight-hour workday. He supported the women's **suffrage** movement and the Nineteenth Amendment, which gave all female citizens the right to vote.

Who led the "petticoat government"?

After Wilson had a stroke in 1919, his wife, Edith, ran the White House. She kept the details of his illness a secret and took care of daily business. With her help, Wilson completed his term, but remained in poor health and died in 1924.

☆ ☆ ☆ ☆ ☆ ☆ ☆ ☆ ☆ ☆

Warren G. Harding
1921–1923

How did "smoke-filled rooms" get Harding elected?

Harding was selected by party leaders to run for president. Many were heavy smokers. They met late at night in secret. By 2:00 in the morning, they made the deal for his nomination.

Did Harding like to play cards?

Yes. He often played poker with cabinet members. In one game, he bet and lost a set of White House dishes!

Why is Harding often ranked as one of the worst U.S. presidents?

His presidency was filled with scandals and corruption. Many of his advisers were dishonest. The greatest scandal—the Teapot Dome affair—took place when a cabinet member sold rights to drill for oil on federal lands in exchange for bribes of money and cattle. Harding died suddenly of a heart attack before Congress could throw him out of office.

Calvin Coolidge
1923–1929

Why was Coolidge so laid-back?

On the sudden death of Harding, Coolidge became president. The country was enjoying economic **prosperity**. Business was booming, so Coolidge took no action: "When things are going along all right, it is a good plan to let them alone."

YOUR PRESIDENTS IQ

What were some of Coolidge's nicknames?

a) "Cal" (short for Calvin)

b) "Red" (for his red hair)

c) "Silent Cal" (he talked little)

d) "Cool" (he was a good dancer)

The answers are a, b, and c. Once, a dinner guest bet "Silent Cal" that she could get him to say "more than three words." Coolidge turned to her and said, "You lose!"

Did Coolidge like to meet with ordinary Americans?

Yes. The president greeted everyone who visited the White House. One day, it took him only thirty-four minutes to shake hands with 1,900 visitors!

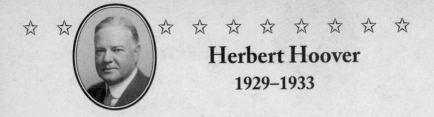

Herbert Hoover
1929–1933

How did Hoover make millions traveling around the world?

He found gold. Hoover made his money as a geologist in the global mining industry. At the start of World War I, he lived in London and helped evacuate 120,000 Americans.

What was the mood of the country when Hoover was elected president in 1928?

Happy. But prosperity came to a sudden end when the **stock market** crashed in October 1929. The country entered the Great Depression as the economy sank. Banks ran out of money, businesses closed, and people lost their jobs.

How bad was the Great Depression?

One out of four people were out of work. Shantytowns of cardboard homes, known as "Hoovervilles," sprung up everywhere as Americans lost their homes. Thousands waited in breadlines for food. Hoover was blamed for the troubles.

Franklin Delano Roosevelt
1933–1945

How did Roosevelt get around the White House?

In a wheelchair. At age thirty-nine, he was suddenly stricken by polio. He lost the use of his legs, which were paralyzed by the disease. Roosevelt learned to stand on leg braces for speeches, but most days he sat at his desk.

How did the president keep busy during his first hundred days in office?

He passed the "New Deal." He signed bills into laws to help the country get out of the Great Depression. Roosevelt reformed the banks and stock market. He built power plants and dams in the Tennessee River.

Roosevelt put people back to work. He also created the **Social Security** system that guaranteed senior citizens some income when they retired.

When did Dr. New Deal become known as "Dr. Win the War"?

FDR called himself Dr. Win the War when the U.S. entered World War II in December 1941. Japan had bombed the U.S. naval base at Pearl Harbor, Hawaii. Roosevelt raised an army of millions of men and women to defeat Hitler's Germany and his allies Italy and Japan.

U.S. factories worked around the clock to turn out war supplies. Women, often for the first time, worked the assembly lines. The U.S. pulled out of the Great Depression, as U.S. soldiers won victory in 1945.

Could you find FDR on the radio or television?

On both. Roosevelt inspired the American people with his radio speeches called "fireside chats." His calm voice comforted them during the difficult days of the Depression and, later, World War II. At the 1939 New York World's Fair, Roosevelt became the first president to appear on TV.

Roosevelt's dog, Fala, went everywhere with the president.

TRUTH! Fala became famous as the "First Dog." The little black Scottie was Roosevelt's faithful companion. The president took Fala with him when he visited the USS *Baltimore*. Sailors aboard the ship tried to cut hair off the dog to keep as souvenirs!

Was First Lady Eleanor Roosevelt a stay-at-home mom?

No. Eleanor and Franklin had five children, but Eleanor worked tirelessly to help people suffering from the Great Depression. She wrote a daily newspaper column and made trips across the country. Eleanor met with poor people, working women, African-Americans, union leaders, and immigrants.

During World War II, Eleanor visited the troops and launched battleships. She was loved and admired. At her peak, the First Lady received 250,000 letters a day and made sure each one was answered.

Did FDR see the end of World War II?

No. On April 12, 1945, Roosevelt fell ill with a headache. He was having a stroke. Roosevelt died within four hours, a month before Germany surrendered.

Only these four presidents have national monuments in Washington, D.C.:

- George Washington
- Thomas Jefferson
- Abraham Lincoln
- Franklin D. Roosevelt

FDR, along with his wife, Eleanor, was honored by a **memorial** built in 1997 in the nation's capital.

How long was Roosevelt president?

FDR completed three full terms and was elected to a fourth. No president previously had served more than two terms. After Roosevelt died, Congress passed an amendment to the Constitution limiting the president to two terms in office.

Harry S. Truman
1945–1953

Who took over when Roosevelt died suddenly in 1945?

Vice President Harry S. Truman. The war in Europe was almost over, but the war against Japan in the Pacific continued.

How did President Truman bring World War II to an end?

The Japanese refused to stop fighting. To save lives, Truman ordered two atomic bombs to be dropped on Japan. The weapons caused many deaths and destroyed two Japanese cities. A few days later, Japan surrendered, and the war was over. More than four hundred thousand Americans had lost their lives in World War II.

What sign was always on Truman's desk?

a) "Speak Softly, Carry a Big Stick"
b) "The Buck Stops Here"
c) "Fair Deal for All"
d) "Hope and Change"

The answer is *b*. The president made the tough decisions. He didn't pass his responsibility to anyone else.

Was Truman elected to a second term?

Yes, but everyone expected him to lose. His opponent, Thomas E. Dewey, was the popular governor of New York. But Truman campaigned hard and surprised the nation by winning.

How did Truman help the countries of Europe after the war?

He supported the Marshall Plan, spending $13 billion to rebuild houses and factories in Europe. At the same time, a "**Cold War**" developed between the U.S. and the Soviet Union. Truman did not trust the Soviet Union and new communist countries.

The president said that the U.S. would help countries trying to stay free of **communism**. His "Truman Doctrine" led the U.S. into war with North Korea in 1950. Later, when asked to help Vietnam fight communists, Truman sent U.S. aid to southeast Asia.

☆ ☆ ☆ ☆ ☆ ☆ ☆ ☆ ☆

Dwight D. Eisenhower
1953–1961

Who liked "Ike"?

Almost everyone. Eisenhower was a popular war hero. As commanding general, he had organized the D-day landing of troops in Europe. He led the Allies to victory in World War II. He won the 1952 election by a landslide.

When he was not in his office, where could you often find President Eisenhower?

On the golf course. Eisenhower built a driving range on the White House lawn so he could practice his golf swing.

How did the U.S. grow during the Eisenhower years?

From forty-eight to fifty states. Alaska and Hawaii joined the union.

The Cold War improved under President Eisenhower.

MYTH! After World War II, America and other free countries were enemies of the Soviet Union and its communist allies. This competition between free democratic countries and those under communism continued under Eisenhower. It got worse when a U.S. spy plane was shot down over Soviet air space. But the president did bring an end to the Korean War.

What race did the U.S. try to win?

The space race. The Soviet Union surprised the world when it launched the first satellite, *Sputnik I*. It was the first man-made object to orbit Earth. Congress set up NASA, the National Aeronautics and Space Administration, to train American scientists and win the space race.

When was President Eisenhower forced to use American troops at home?

In 1957, to end the **segregation**, or separation, of black and white students in U.S. schools. The governor of Arkansas tried to stop black students from going to an all-white public school. The president ordered federal troops to Arkansas so that students could enter the school safely.

John F. Kennedy
1961–1963

How did John F. Kennedy use TV to get elected?

Kennedy won over voters with his good looks and performance on televised debates against his opponent, Richard Nixon.

TRUTH or MYTH?

Kennedy always wished to be president.

MYTH! Actually, he thought about becoming a writer. But Joseph Kennedy, JFK's millionaire father, wanted one of his four sons to become president. When the oldest son, Joe Jr., died in World War II, it was up to John ("Jack") to fulfill his father's dream.

What happened to Kennedy's boat during World War II?

While Kennedy was serving as a naval lieutenant, his boat was shot by a Japanese warship and sank. Kennedy swam for four hours. He pulled along an injured sailor by grabbing the man's life-jacket strap in his teeth. Kennedy was awarded a medal for his bravery.

How did Kennedy bring young people to politics?

By his words. Kennedy was an energetic campaigner, promising to get the country moving again. In his 1961 Inaugural Address, he inspired a new generation: "Ask not what your country can do for you—ask what you can do for your country."

What did Kennedy promise to do by the end of the 1960s?

To put a man on the moon. Kennedy was a big supporter of space exploration. He called space "the new frontier."

Who accompanied First Lady Jackie Kennedy to Paris?

President Kennedy. His young wife spoke French fluently and was more popular than the president in Europe. Women the world over copied her speech and the clothes she wore. She brought movie-star glamour to the White House.

Why didn't Kennedy finish his first term?

The president was shot and killed in Dallas, Texas, on November 22, 1963. Police arrested Lee Harvey Oswald, but he was killed two days later by another man. To this day, people are not sure exactly what happened that day. But the young president was dead and a nation mourned.

Kennedy's funeral was on television. With tears in their eyes, Americans watched as the president's three-year-old son saluted his father's coffin.

Did John Kennedy and Martin Luther King, Jr., share the same dream?

Yes, they both wanted equal rights and justice for African-Americans. Kennedy proposed the civil rights law, which Congress passed after his death. King's "I Have a Dream" speech was heard by two hundred thousand marchers in Washington, D.C., in August 1963.

☆ ☆ ☆ ☆ ☆ ☆ ☆ ☆ ☆ ☆ ☆

Lyndon B. Johnson

1963–1969

How long did it take Lyndon Johnson to become president after Kennedy's death?

Only a few hours. As vice president, Johnson was sworn in as president aboard Air Force One, the presidential jet, just after Kennedy's assassination. Mrs. Johnson and Jackie Kennedy looked on, as the new president took the oath of office.

TRUTH or MYTH?

Johnson was a big man from a small state.

MYTH! At six feet three inches, Johnson was tall, but he was from Texas, the second-*largest* state. Growing up in poverty, Johnson worked hard to get a college education. He never forgot the poor Mexican-American children he taught in rural Texas. Johnson had a dream to one day create a "Great Society" without poverty and racial hatred.

Did Johnson declare war in America?

Yes, and his "War on Poverty" improved the lives of many poor people. As president, he passed many laws to strengthen education, create public housing, secure voting rights for minorities, and increase health care for the poor and elderly.

How did Johnson's nickname become a family tradition?

All the Johnsons had "LBJ" initials:
- Lady Bird Johnson, his wife
- Lynda Bird and Luci Baines Johnson, his daughters
- Little Beagle Johnson, his dog

Who did Johnson appoint to the Supreme Court in 1967?

Thurgood Marshall, the first African-American to serve on the nation's highest court.

Why did Johnson not run for reelection in 1968?

He knew he would lose. Johnson was a popular president in 1964, but he was forced out of the race by 1967. He had supported the Vietnam War with bombs and troops. At one point, more than five hundred thousand U.S. soldiers were fighting there. Angry citizens took to the streets in protest. Americans wanted the country out of Vietnam and Johnson out of office.

Richard M. Nixon
1969–1974

Did Nixon have a lot of government jobs?

Yes. During World War II, he served in the U.S. Navy. Nixon was elected to Congress in 1950 and was Eisenhower's vice president for eight years.

Nixon lost the presidential race of 1960 to John F. Kennedy. He quit politics in 1962, only to return to win the presidential election of 1968.

How did Nixon get the nickname "Tricky Dick"?

Because of the way he won elections. His critics said Nixon used illegal campaign funds and attacked the character of his opponent to win his Senate seat in 1950. When he ran as Eisenhower's vice president, Nixon gave his famous "Checkers speech." He admitted to Americans on TV that his dog, Checkers, had been a gift from a campaign contributor. His emotional speech helped improve his image.

TRUTH or MYTH?

Burglars, hired by Nixon's closest advisers, were caught stealing from the Watergate Hotel in Washington, D.C.

TRUTH! The men were there to steal papers from President Nixon's political opponents. But they were caught. Nixon tried to cover up the illegal break-in. It became a scandal. Secret tape recordings at the White House showed that Nixon had lied. The president was forced to resign from office, or Congress would impeach him and make him leave.

"I am not a crook," Nixon told the American people in a press conference. He left the White House on August 9, 1974, in disgrace.

What were some of Nixon's achievements in office? He:

a) negotiated an end to the Vietnam War.

b) spoke to U.S. astronauts who landed on the moon.

c) made the first trip to China by a U.S. president.

d) lowered the voting age from twenty-one to eighteen.

All of the above. Nixon had many successes, but sadly he is remembered as the first president to resign from office.

Gerald R. Ford
1974–1977

As the elected vice president, Gerald Ford became president when Nixon resigned in 1974.

MYTH! Ford did replace Nixon, but he was never elected as vice president or president. He was the first president to hold the office without being elected to either office. Nixon had appointed Ford when his first vice president, Spiro Agnew, resigned after a scandal in 1973.

Ford was an all-star college football player. How good was he?

Very good. Ford had offers to play professional football, but he wanted to be a lawyer. To pay for his tuition at Yale Law School, he worked as a fashion model.

Ford was a slow speaker. One time, he fell stepping out of Air Force One. Some critics meanly joked that Ford had played "too long without a helmet."

Why was President Ford nicknamed "Mr. Nice Guy"?

Ford tried to heal the country after the Watergate scandal. He gave **amnesty**, or forgiveness, to Vietnam War deserters. Ford even granted Nixon a presidential pardon for his crimes.

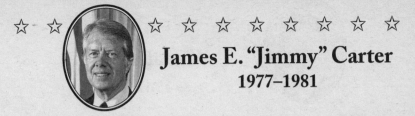

James E. "Jimmy" Carter
1977–1981

Did James Earl Carter, Jr., like his name?

No. Carter liked the name "Jimmy" better. He was sworn in as President "Jimmy" Carter

He went to the U.S. Naval Academy and trained as a nuclear engineer. When his father died, Carter took over the family's peanut farm in Georgia.

Why did Carter get elected in 1976?

After the Watergate scandal, voters liked "the outsider" from the South. He campaigned hard and got elected.

Did he get a second term?

No. In 1979, angry Iranians held fifty-two American hostages in the U.S. Embassy in Tehran. Americans blamed Carter. After 444 days, the hostages were finally released. It was Carter's last day in office.

TRUTH or MYTH?

President Carter was more popular out of office than in.

TRUTH! Only fifty-six when he left office, Carter went on to a career in charitable and diplomatic work. He has written over twenty books, and received the Nobel Peace Prize in 2002.

Ronald Reagan
1981–1989

When did President Reagan celebrate his seventieth birthday?

Just sixteen days after he took the oath of office. He was the oldest person to become president. Reagan enjoyed horseback riding and had a happy, optimistic nature.

Why was Reagan known as the "Great Communicator"?

Because he was relaxed in front of the camera. Reagan moved to Hollywood in 1937 and became a movie actor. He made more than fifty movies. Before becoming president, Reagan had also been a TV host and governor of California.

Did Reagan have a sweet tooth?

Probably. He kept a jar of jelly beans on his desk and passed it around at meetings.

JELLY BEANS

When did the president "dodge a bullet"?

A few months after taking office, Reagan was shot by a mentally ill man. Doctors removed a bullet from the president's lungs. Reagan joked: "I forgot to duck!"

What did "Reaganomics" do for the economy?

a) Created **welfare** programs for the poor

b) Cut taxes for the rich

c) Allocated more money for defense

d) Ensured health care for the elderly

The answers are *b* and *c*. Reagan said that tax cuts for business would "trickle down" money from wealthy people and help poorer citizens. Over time, there *were* more jobs, but there also was a bank crisis. The national debt doubled by 1980.

What did Reagan always ask the voters?

"Are you better off than you were four years ago?" asked Reagan in his first campaign. Most voters answered "no" because of the bad economy under Jimmy Carter. The popular Reagan was easily elected to two terms.

George H. W. Bush
1989–1993

Was President Bush "born with a silver spoon in his mouth"?

Yes, say his critics. The president came from a rich family. Bush went to private schools and attended Yale University. He held many government jobs, such as U.S. Ambassador to the United Nations, before becoming Reagan's vice president.

TRUTH or MYTH?

Bush had a fear of flying.

MYTH! He liked airplanes—and jumping out of them! During World War II, Bush became the navy's youngest pilot at nineteen. He flew bombing missions in the Pacific. Four years after leaving the White House, the elderly Bush made a parachute jump just for fun.

What vegetable *wasn't* on the White House menu?

Broccoli. Bush refused to eat it. Angry growers sent truckloads of broccoli to the White House in protest.

Did Bush get the country into war?

Yes, but the wars were short and successful. In 1989, U.S. troops invaded Panama to capture the country's corrupt leader. A year later, the U.S. and its allies launched Operation Desert Storm against Saddam Hussein. The Iraqi leader had invaded Kuwait, its oil-rich neighbor in the Persian Gulf.

What was Bush's record on the environment?

Good. He warned about global warming. In 1992, Bush signed the Earth Pledge in Rio de Janeiro, limiting the emission of **greenhouse gases** into the atmosphere.

In 1989, the oil tanker *Exxon Valdez* ran aground. Almost eleven million gallons of oil spilled off the shore of Alaska. Thousands of birds and animals were killed.

Why did candidate Bush ask voters to "read my lips"?

He made voters a promise: "Read my lips: no new taxes." But he broke that promise and raised taxes when the economy got worse. Bush lost the 1992 election, after one term in office.

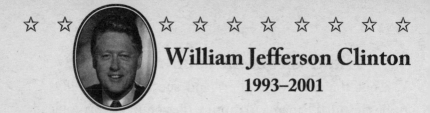

William Jefferson Clinton
1993–2001

What did Bill Clinton wish for as a child?

To be president. Young Bill ran for every high-school office until his principal wouldn't let him try for any more. When he was sixteen, Clinton shook hands with President Kennedy at a White House meeting for future leaders.

Did Clinton play any special sport?

Clinton liked to run, but he *really* liked to play the saxophone. He was so talented that he was offered music scholarships after high school. Clinton played his saxophone on TV shows when running for president in 1992.

The American economy got worse during the Clinton years.

MYTH! It was a time of peace and prosperity. Clinton balanced the budget. He signed free trade agreements, opened up trade with China, and improved relations with Russia. But Clinton battled with Congress over taxes and trade. He made many enemies during his two terms in office.

Did Clinton marry his law-school study partner?

Yes. He met his future wife, Hillary Rodham, at Yale University. "If you elect Bill, you get me," she said. Hillary became a popular First Lady. She worked to try to fix the nation's health care system, fought for the rights of children, and traveled the world to represent her husband.

Hillary became the first former First Lady to win public office. Elected to the Senate in 2000, she ran for president herself in 2008.

Why was Clinton called the "Comeback Kid"?

When Clinton was governor, he was not reelected. He ran the next time, and became governor again in 1982. Clinton became known as the "Comeback Kid." He had to fight for reelection as president, too. The other party had won control of Congress in 1994. But the U.S. economy was strong. Clinton campaigned hard and won again in 1996.

TRUTH or MYTH?

Congress voted to impeach President Clinton and put him on trial.

TRUTH! Clinton was charged by Congress with breaking the law. He was accused of lying to hide a romantic relationship with a White House intern. Clinton admitted his guilt. He was tried by the Senate and acquitted. Clinton kept his job and completed his second term.

Many voters supported Clinton. Despite the scandal, he remains a popular former president. Clinton works hard to promote peace and human rights throughout the world.

George W. Bush
2001–2009

Why did it take thirty-six days for George W. Bush to be named winner of the 2000 election?

The 2000 election between Texas governor George Bush and Vice President Al Gore was "too close to call." More people voted for Gore, but Bush won the electoral vote—the one that mattered. It took a recount of certain votes in Florida and a decision by the Supreme Court for Bush to win.

Why was Bush nicknamed "W" and "43"?

To tell him apart from his father, George Herbert Walker Bush, the nation's forty-first president. Some people called the presidents "number 41" and "number 43." Usually, they referred to the younger Bush as "W," which stands for *Walker*, his middle name.

BUSH WAS THE SON OF A FORMER PRESIDENT.

SO WAS JOHN QUINCY ADAMS.

What terrible event on September 11, 2001, marked the Bush presidency?

The worst attack ever by **terrorists** in America. Four planes were hijacked by al-Qaeda, a terrorist group. Two of the airplanes destroyed the 110-story World Trade Center twin towers in New York City. Another plane crashed into the Pentagon, and the fourth plane crashed in a Pennsylvania field on its way to Washington, D.C. Almost three thousand Americans were killed.

To fight back against the terrorists, Bush sent U.S. troops to Afghanistan. On March 20, 2003, the U.S. invaded Iraq.

TRUTH or MYTH?

On May 1, 2003, Bush landed by navy jet on the USS *Abraham Lincoln*. A banner behind the president declared "Mission accomplished."

TRUTH! The president, wearing a flight suit, landed on the deck of the aircraft carrier. But the Iraq War was far from over. U.S. troops were still in Iraq after George Bush left office. It was a long and costly war.

How did Bush bring big changes to America's schools?

A law called "No Child Left Behind" was passed. All states were required to test fourth-grade students' math and reading skills. Students spent hours each week preparing for the tests.

What natural disaster happened at home in 2005?

Hurricane Katrina. New Orleans, Louisiana, a major city on the Gulf of Mexico, was severely flooded. Winds over a hundred miles an hour had broken the levees holding back the water. Many people lost their lives and property.

Did Bush keep his campaign promise and cut everyone's taxes?

Yes. But with lower taxes, the government didn't collect enough revenue. The wars cost a lot, and the economy was slowing down. At the end of Bush's presidency, there was a financial crisis that almost caused another Great Depression.

Barack Obama
2009–present

What happened on August 28, 2008, forty-five years to the day after Dr. King's "I Have a Dream" speech?

Barack Obama accepted his party's nomination for president. He became the nation's first African-American president. Obama's mother was a white woman from Kansas, and his father, a black African from Kenya.

What election did Obama win at Harvard Law School?

He was chosen to head the *Harvard Law Review*, the first African-American to achieve this honor.

Who listened to Obama's campaign calls of "Yes We Can"?

The majority of voters. Obama easily won the election of 2008. He was an attractive candidate who appealed to young people, many voting for the first time.

What jobs did Obama have before he ran for president?

a) College professor
b) Author
c) Community organizer
d) Civil-rights lawyer
e) U.S. Senator

All of the above. Obama has authored two books, *Dreams from My Father* and *The Audacity of Hope*. Both were bestsellers.

Where did President Obama learn to surf?

In Hawaii. He was raised there by his mother and grandparents.

How did President Obama meet his wife, Michelle?

They worked together at a Chicago law firm. Married in 1992, the Obamas have two daughters. Malia and Sasha were only ten and seven years old when their father took office and moved their family to the White House.

How was Obama treated as a "superstar" on the political scene?

Since 2004, when he gave a speech at the Democratic convention, Obama became the young star of the party. His face appeared on T-shirts and magazine covers.

Obama had tough competition from Hillary Clinton when he ran for president in 2008. But he pulled ahead in the primary voting to win his party's nomination. After his election, President Obama appointed Hillary Clinton to his cabinet as Secretary of State.

Who else besides Obama stood on the steps of the Illinois old state capitol building to announce his candidacy for president?

Abraham Lincoln. Both faced a major crisis when in office. Lincoln had to fight the Civil War to keep the nation together. Obama had to get the country out of two wars in Iraq and Afghanistan and head off a financial depression.

What big economic problem did Obama face after taking office?

A financial mess. The banks were in crisis. The automobile industry was bankrupt. Too many Americans were losing their homes and jobs. Obama's quick actions to "stimulate" the economy helped keep America from falling into a depression.

What action did Obama take on May 2, 2011, that surprised the world?

Obama sent Navy SEAL Team Six, U.S. Special Operations fighters, on a dangerous mission into Abbottabad, Pakistan. Landing by helicopters just after midnight, the U.S. forces stormed the house where the al-Qaeda terrorist leader Osama bin Laden had been hiding.

It took more than ten years for American intelligence to track down bin Laden, but only minutes for the SEALs to find and kill him. His body was taken away and buried at sea. Many Americans supported the death of bin Laden, the mastermind behind the 9/11 attacks.

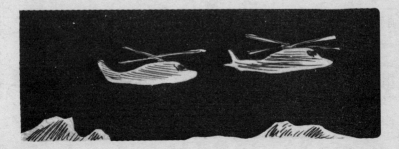

❧ *Appendix* ❧

Presidents and Their Vice Presidents

Election Year	President Vice President	Term
1789, 1792	**George Washington** John Adams	**1789–1797** 1789–1797
1796	**John Adams** Thomas Jefferson	**1797–1801** 1797–1801
1800, 1804	**Thomas Jefferson** Aaron Burr George Clinton	**1801–1809** 1801–1805 1805–1809
1808, 1812	**James Madison** George Clinton Elbridge Gerry*	**1809–1817** 1809–1812 1812–1814
1816, 1820	**James Monroe** Daniel D. Tompkins	**1817–1825** 1817–1825
1824	**John Quincy Adams** John C. Calhoun	**1825–1829** 1825–1829
1828, 1832	**Andrew Jackson** John C. Calhoun Martin Van Buren	**1829–1837** 1829–1832 1833–1837

*Died in office and not replaced.

1836	**Martin Van Buren**	**1837–1841**
	Richard M. Johnsona	1837–1841
1840	**William Henry Harrison**	**1841**
	John Tyler	1841
	John Tyler	**1841–1845**
1844	**James K. Polk**	**1845-1849**
	George M. Dallas	1845–1849
1848	**Zachary Taylor**	**1849–1850**
	Millard Fillmore	1849–1850
	Millard Fillmore	**1850–1853**
1852	**Franklin Pierce**	**1853–1857**
	William R. King*	1853
1856	**James Buchanan**	**1857–1861**
	John C. Breckinridge	1857–1861
1860, 1864	**Abraham Lincoln**	**1861–1865**
	Hannibal Hamlin	1861–1865
	Andrew Johnson	1865
	Andrew Johnson	**1865–1869**
1868, 1872	**Ulysses S. Grant**	**1869–1877**
	Schuyler Colfax	1869–1873
	Henry Wilson*	1873–1875

1876	**Rutherford B. Hayes**	**1877–1881**
	William A. Wheeler	1877–1881
1880	**James A. Garfield**	**1881**
	Chester A. Arthur	1881
	Chester A. Arthur	**1881–1885**
1884	**Grover Cleveland**	**1885–1889**
	Thomas A. Hendricks*	1885
1888	**Benjamin Harrison**	**1889–1893**
	Levi P. Morton	1889–1893
1892	**Grover Cleveland**	**1893–1897**
	Adlai E. Stevenson	1893–1897
1896, 1900	**William McKinley**	**1897–1901**
	Garret A. Hobart+	1897–1899
	Theodore Roosevelt	1901
1904	**Theodore Roosevelt**	**1901–1909**
	Charles W. Fairbanks	1905–1909
1908	**William Howard Taft**	**1909–1913**
	James S. Sherman	1909–1912
1912, 1916	**Woodrow Wilson**	**1913–1921**
	Thomas R. Marshall	1913–1921
1920	**Warren G. Harding**	**1921–1923**
	Calvin Coolidge	1921–1923

*Died in office and not replaced.
+Died in office.

1924	**Calvin Coolidge**	**1923–1929**
	Charles G. Dawes	1925–1929
1928	**Herbert Hoover**	**1929–1933**
	Charles Curtis	1929–1933
1932, 1936,	**Franklin Delano Roosevelt**	**1933–1945**
1940, 1944	John N. Garner	1933–1941
	Henry A. Wallace	1941–1945
	Harry S. Truman	1945
1948	**Harry S. Truman**	**1945–1953**
	Alben W. Barkley	1949–1953
1952, 1956	**Dwight D. Eisenhower**	**1953–1961**
	Richard M. Nixon	1953–1961
1960	**John F. Kennedy**	**1961–1963**
	Lyndon B. Johnson	1961–1963
1964	**Lyndon B. Johnson**	**1963–1969**
	Hubert H. Humphrey	1965–1969
1968, 1972	**Richard M. Nixon**	**1969–1974**
	Spiro Agnew	1969–1973
	Gerald R. Ford	1973–1974
	Gerald R. Ford	**1974–1977**
	Nelson A. Rockefeller	1974–1977
1976	**Jimmy Carter**	**1977–1981**
	Walter F. Mondale	1977–1981

1980, 1984	**Ronald Reagan**	**1981–1989**
	George H.W. Bush	1981–1989
1988	**George H.W. Bush**	**1989–1993**
	J. Danforth Quayle	1989–1993
1992, 1996	**William Jefferson Clinton**	**1993–2001**
	Albert Gore, Jr.	1993–2001
2000, 2004	**George W. Bush**	**2001–2009**
	Richard B. Cheney	2001–2009
2008, 2012	**Barack Obama**	**2009–**
	Joseph Biden, Jr.	2009–

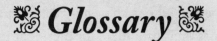 Glossary

abolitionist – a person who supported the end of slavery

ambassador – a person who represents his or her country in another country

amendment – an addition or change to the U.S. Constitution

amnesty – a decision by a government to forgive, and not punish, a person who commits an illegal act

assassinate – to murder a famous person for political reasons

assembly – a group of people gathered together for a particular purpose

civil service – government departments not belonging to the military

Cold War – the unfriendly competition for power and influence between the United States and the Soviet Union that developed after World War II

communism – an economic system based on public ownership of property

compromise – an agreement between two sides with different opinions, in which each side gives up something it wanted

document – a piece of paper with official information on it

elector – a person who is chosen by voters in a particular state to support their candidate for president in the voting of the Electoral College

Emancipation Proclamation – an official document made by President Abraham Lincoln in 1863 that freed the slaves in Confederate states

global – related to the whole world

greenhouse gas – a gas produced when carbon burns that is trapped in Earth's atmosphere and causes gradual warming of the Earth

immigrant – a person who comes into a foreign country in order to live there

impeach – to accuse formally a public official of a serious crime related to his or her job

inauguration – the ceremony that puts a person into an official position

independence – when a country has its own government and is not ruled by another country

isolation – the separation, or keeping apart, of one nation from other nations

memorial – a statue or building made to honor a person or event

monopoly – complete control of a particular good or service

naturalist – a person who studies plants and animals

Nobel Prize – international prizes given each year to people who make important discoveries or contributions in science, economics, literature, and peace

oath – a serious promise to tell the truth or to do what you have said

panic – a sudden strong fear that prevents people from acting in a calm manner

pedometer – a device that measures how far a person has walked

political party – a group that organizes to support a particular plan of action and to offer candidates for elected office

primary election – a first election, or series of elections, in which voters of each party nominate candidates for office

prosperity – a time when people of a country enjoy financial success

radical – a person who believes that there should be great political or economic change

ration – a limited amount of something that one person is allowed to have

reconstruct—to rebuild and join again the former Confederate states into the Union after the Civil War

scandal—immoral actions that cause other people to react with shock or anger

segregation—the act or practice of keeping one group of people apart from others because of race or religion

Social Security—a government program that gives financial help for the elderly and people unable to work

stock market—place where shares (parts of ownership of companies) are bought and sold

suffrage—the right to vote in an election

temperance—the habit of avoiding extreme behavior, such as not drinking too much alcohol

terrorist—a person who acts violently for political purposes

veto—the power to refuse to allow something to happen

welfare—the system in which the government pays for health care and other benefits for its citizens